WAR PLANES

Carrier-Based Jet Fighters:
The F-14 Tomcats
by Michael and Gladys Green

CAPSTONE
HIGH-INTEREST
BOOKS

an imprint of Capstone Press
Mankato, Minnesota

Capstone High-Interest Books are published by Capstone Press
151 Good Counsel Drive, P.O. Box 669, Mankato, Minnesota 56002
http://www.capstone-press.com

Library of Congress Cataloging-in-Publication Data
Green, Michael, 1952—
    Carrier-based jet fighters: the F-14 Tomcats / by Michael Green and Gladys Green.
    p. cm.—(War planes)
    Summary: Discusses the design and weapons of three models of the F-14 Tomcat
fighter jet and how they are used by the Navy.
    Includes bibliographical references and index.
    ISBN 0-7368-2149-X (hardcover)
    1. Tomcat (Jet fighter plane)—Juvenile literature. [1. Tomcat (Jet fighter plane) 2.
Fighter planes. 3. Airplanes, Military.] I. Green, Gladys, 1954–II. Title. III. Series.
UG1242.F5.G7126 2004
623.7'464—dc21   2002155929

Editorial Credits
Christine Peterson, editor; Timothy Halldin, series designer; Patrick Dentinger, book
    designer; Jo Miller, photo researcher; Eric Kudalis, product planning editor

Photo Credits
Defense Visual Information Center, cover, 1, 13, 16–17, 18, 20, 23
Navy Photo by PH1 Martin Maddock, 9; PHAN Matthew Keane, 24; Ensign
    Charles M. Abell, 29
Ted Carlson/Fotodynamics, 4, 7, 10, 26

Consultant
Raymond L. Puffer, Ph.D., Historian, Air Force Flight Test Center, Edwards Air
Force Base, California

1 2 3 4 5 6 08 07 06 05 04 03

Table of Contents

Chapter 1 The F-14 in Action 5

Chapter 2 Inside the F-14 11

Chapter 3 Weapons and Tactics 19

Chapter 4 The Future 27

Features

F-14A Specifications 15

Photo Diagram 16

Words to Know 30

To Learn More 31

Useful Addresses 31

Internet Sites 32

Index 32

Chapter One

Learn About

- The F-14s on patrol
- F-14 development
- F-14 models

The F-14 in Action

Two U.S. Navy F-14 Tomcats patrol the skies above the Indian Ocean. The F-14 crews are looking for enemy planes that may attack the aircraft carrier where the Tomcats are based. Leaders of an enemy country warned of an attack against the U.S. warships.

A radar operator on board the F-14 sees six enemy planes on the radar screen. The planes are 200 miles (320 kilometers) away and approaching fast. The F-14 crews learn that the enemy planes are armed with antiship missiles.

The F-14 pilots fire six long-range missiles at the enemy planes. Radar guides the missiles. Four enemy planes are quickly shot down. The pilots in the remaining enemy planes fire their missiles at the Navy carrier. Pilots in the F-14s fire more missiles and destroy the enemy weapons in the air. The last two enemy pilots turn their planes around and retreat.

The U.S. pilots turn their jets back toward the carrier. On the way back, the pilots spot an enemy patrol boat. The boat is armed with antiship missiles. F-14 pilots use the plane's guns to sink the enemy ship. The F-14 pilots safely return their planes to the carrier.

About the F-14

In 1967, the U.S. Navy began plans for a new two-seat jet. The new plane would take off from Navy aircraft carriers. The jet would guard the carriers from enemy attacks.

A pilot and radar operator make up the F-14 crew.

The Navy chose the Northrop Grumman Corporation to build the plane. Northrop Grumman called its new plane the F-14 Tomcat. The F-14A was the first Tomcat model. Northrop Grumman made 557 F-14As for the Navy.

Pilots took the F-14A on its first test flight in December 1970. The Navy began using the F-14A two years later.

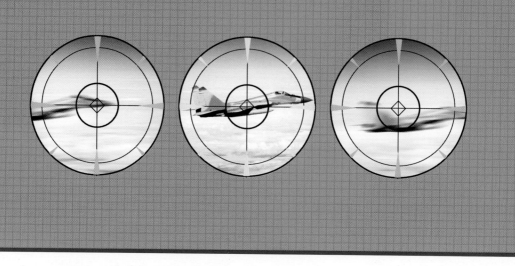

New F-14 Models

Northrop Grumman built three models of the F-14 for the Navy. The F-14B entered service in 1987. This plane had a more powerful engine.

The F-14D is the most recent and advanced model of the Tomcat. Built in 1988, this plane has a better avionics system than other models. Avionics include the radar, radios, flight controls, navigation, and fire control systems.

There are other differences between the three F-14 models. The F-14B and F-14D models have a larger engine exhaust than the F-14A. A dual chin pod was put under the nose of the F-14D. This piece of equipment has sensors that improve the plane's radar.

All F-14s are stationed on U.S. Navy carriers.

Chapter Two

Learn About

- F-14 engines
- Variable-Geometry wings
- F-14 radar

Inside the F-14

The F-14 uses its moveable wings and jet engines to travel faster than the speed of sound. The F-14 has a top speed of 1,544 miles (2,485 kilometers) per hour.

Some F-14 models have different features. The F-14D has a newer engine. This model of the F-14 also uses an advanced radar system.

All models of the plane have an advanced weapons system. F-14 pilots use this system to keep track of 24 targets at the same time.

Engines

The F-14A has two Pratt & Whitney TF30 jet engines. Each engine produces 20,900 pounds (9,480 kilograms) of thrust. Thrust is the force that pushes a jet plane forward.

The F-14B and F-14D models have a more powerful engine than the F-14A. The newer General Electric F110 engine can produce 27,000 pounds (12,247 kilograms) of thrust. The newer F110 engine uses less fuel than the older TF30 engine. With the new engine, F-14B and F-14D jets have a range of more than 3,000 miles (4,828 kilometers).

Moveable Wings

The wings of the F-14 move forward or backward when the plane changes its speed. This ability is called variable-geometry (VG) or "swing-wing." F-14 pilots use swing-wing to change the distance between the plane's two wings. The F-14 has a wingspan of 64 feet, 1 inch (20 meters) when its wings are moved forward. With its wings swept back, the jet's wingspan is 38 feet, 2 inches (12 meters).

The F-14's wings sweep back so the jet can fly faster.

The F-14's wings sweep back when the plane needs to go faster. The F-14 can travel faster than the speed of sound with its wings swept all the way back.

A computer controls the F-14's wings while in flight. The computer picks the best sweep angle for the plane's wings. In flight, the F-14's wings have a sweep angle between 20 and 68 degrees.

The F-14's wings are at a 20-degree sweep angle during takeoffs and landings when the plane needs to have high lift.

Cockpit

The F-14's pilot and radar intercept officer (RIO) sit in the plane's cockpit. The RIO controls the radar and sensor systems. These systems find and follow targets. The RIO aims the plane's weapons at a target. The pilot fires the weapons.

A large canopy covers the F-14 cockpit. The F-14's crew can see around most of the plane through the clear canopy.

The head-up display (HUD) allows the pilot to keep track of the plane's systems. This small screen is located in the cockpit. The HUD shows data about the plane's speed, altitude, weapons, and targets.

Radar

F-14s use different radar systems to track enemy planes. The F-14A and F-14B use the Avionics Weapons Group (AWG-9). This system is located in the nose of these planes.

The AWG-9 can find large planes that are 230 miles (370 kilometers) away. The system finds smaller planes when they are about 131 miles (211 kilometers) away. AWG-9 finds antiship missiles that are 74 miles (119 kilometers) away.

F-14A Specifications

Function:	Fighter Interceptor
Manufacturer:	Northrop Grumman Corporation
Date Deployed:	1972
Length:	61 feet, 9 inches (18.8 meters)
Wingspan:	64 feet, 1 inch (20 meters) unswept
Height:	16 feet (4.9 meters)
Weight:	40,104 pounds (18,191 kilograms) without fuel or weapons
Engine:	Two Pratt & Whitney TF30 jet engines
Speed:	1,544 miles (2,485 kilometers) per hour
Range:	2,000 miles (3,219 kilometers) without refueling
Ceiling:	56,000 feet (17,069 meters)

The F-14D model has a newer airborne radar system called the APG-71. This system has a longer range than the AWG-9. With the APG-71, the F-14D can find targets that are farther away. The APG-71's top range remains a Navy secret.

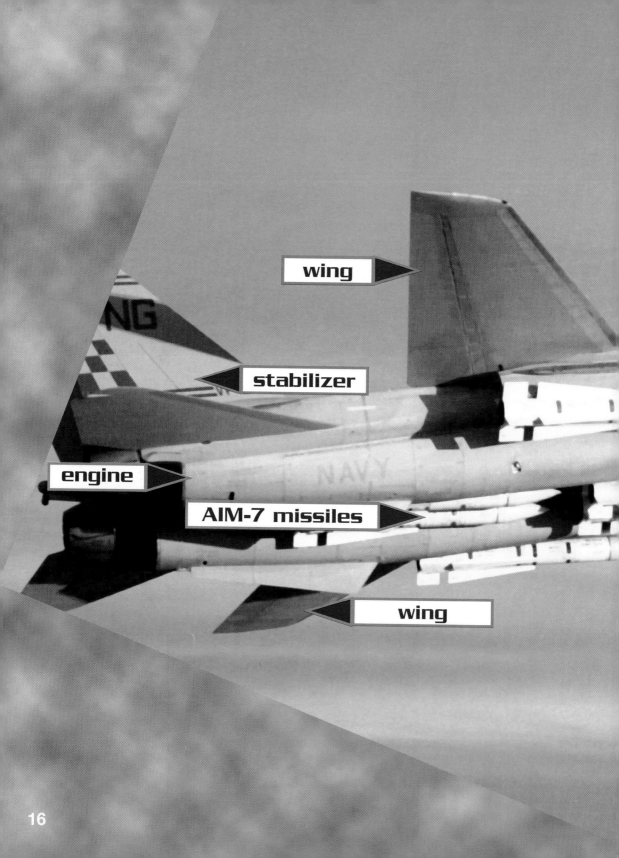

wing

stabilizer

engine

AIM-7 missiles

wing

The F-14 Tomcat

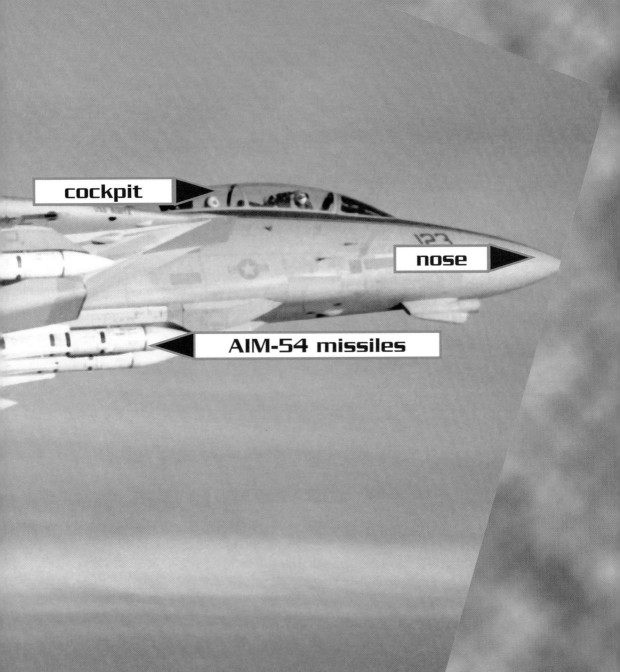

cockpit

nose

AIM-54 missiles

Chapter Three

Learn About

- F-14 missiles
- Short-range weapons
- LANTIRN System

Weapons and Tactics

The F-14's main mission is to protect U.S. Navy carriers from enemy attack. F-14 crews use different weapons during combat. All of the F-14's weapons can hit targets at different ranges.

The F-14 carries three types of air-to-air missiles. The F-14 crew uses these missiles against enemy planes during combat.

In 1995, some F-14s were changed to carry different types of bombs. These planes were called "Bombcats."

An F-14 crew fires an AIM-54 missile.

AIM-54 Phoenix

The AIM-54 Phoenix is the F-14's main
air intercept missile (AIM). The AIM-54
hits targets with a 135-pound (61-kilogram)
high-explosive warhead. This missile can hit
targets that are 115 miles (185 kilometers) away.

The AIM-54 can hit enemy planes that fly at low or high altitudes. The AIM-54 is powered by a rocket motor. This missile has a top speed of 3,000 miles (4,828 kilometers) per hour.

The AIM-54 is a large missile. The missile is 13 feet (4 meters) long with a diameter of 15 inches (38 centimeters). The AIM-54 weighs 1,108 pounds (503 kilograms). Because of its size and weight, Navy carrier crews call the AIM-54 missile the "Buffalo." On a normal mission, the F-14 carries four AIM-54 missiles under its main body.

The F-14's radar system finds the enemy target. The pilot then launches an AIM-54. After it is launched, the AIM-54 uses the F-14's radar system to find its target. When the AIM-54 is 14 miles (23 kilometers) away, the missile switches to its own radar system. The AIM-54 changes radar systems to protect the F-14 from enemy attack.

AIM-7 Sparrow

Some F-14 combat missions require missiles that can hit targets at shorter distances. The F-14 uses AIM-7 Sparrow missiles on these missions. The 500-pound (227-kilogram) AIM-7 is 12 feet (3.7 meters) long. The missile's body is 8 inches (20 centimeters) in diameter.

AIM-9 Sidewinder

The F-14 pilots also use the AIM-9 Sidewinder missile. This missile is more than 9 feet (2.7 meters) long with a diameter of only 5 inches (12.7 centimeters). The AIM-9 weighs 200 pounds (91 kilograms). The missile can hit targets up to 10 miles (16 kilometers) away.

Bombs and Guns

Laser-guided bombs (LGBs) are the most common bomb dropped by the F-14 pilots. Each LGB has a sensor that can see laser light bouncing off a target. The LGB's sensor uses this light to guide the bomb.

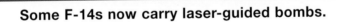

Some F-14s now carry laser-guided bombs.

The F-14 is equipped with a six-barrel 20-millimeter automatic cannon called the M61A1 Vulcan. F-14 pilots use this gun on targets that are 1 mile (1.6 kilometers) away.

Crews load bullets into the M61A1 cannon.

LANTIRN Pod

A targeting system helps the F-14 drop bombs at night. The Low Altitude Navigation and Targeting Infrared for Night (LANTIRN) is carried in two large pods under the F-14's wings.

One pod has a Forward-Looking Infrared (FLIR) camera. This camera uses heat from objects to make a picture. The picture shows the F-14's crew what is happening outside the plane.

The other pod has a Global Positioning System (GPS). This system uses data from 24 satellites in space. The satellites circle the Earth. The F-14 picks up signals from the satellites. The pilot uses this data to see the exact position of the plane.

Chapter Four

Learn About

- F-14 replacement
- F-14 improvements
- Night vision goggles

The Future

The F-14 has been a top jet fighter for many years. Only 200 Tomcats are still in use. The Navy plans to retire the F-14A by 2004 and F-14B by 2007. The Navy plans to retire the last Tomcat, the F-14D, in 2008. The F/A-18 Super Hornet will replace the Tomcat on U.S. Navy carriers.

Over the years, the Navy has updated the F-14. These updates include more advanced electronic sensors.

TV and Infrared Cameras

The Navy put a TV Camera System (TCS) in some F-14 models. The TCS uses closed-circuit TV and long-range lenses to find enemy planes and ships. The TCS uses a long-range camera lens to find targets. This system can only be used during the day.

The F-14D is fitted with the TCS and an Infrared Search and Track (IRST) sensor. F-14D crews can use this system day or night, and in any type of weather. F-14 crews can see pictures from the TCS and IRST systems on a small screen in the cockpit.

Night Vision Goggles

In 1996, F-14 crews began wearing night vision goggles (NVGs). The NVGs look like binoculars. Flight crews wear them on their helmets. NVGs collect light from the stars, the Moon, and other objects. Flight crews can see a picture made by the light.

The F-14 takes off from short runways on carriers.

The F-14 will use its updated equipment and sensors to remain a top fighter jet. The Navy uses the Tomcat for carrier air defense, jet escorts, and ground attacks. The F-14 remains an important part of the Navy's defense plans.

Words to Know

exhaust (eg-ZAWST)—heated air leaving a jet engine

infrared system (IN-fruh-red SISS-tuhm)—machinery that detects objects by the heat they give off

laser beam (LAY-zur BEEM)—a narrow intense beam of light

mission (MISH-uhn)—a military task

radar (RAY-dar)—equipment that uses radio waves to locate and guide objects

satellite (SAT-uh-lite)—a spacecraft that circles around Earth; satellites are used to gather and send information.

sensor (SEN-sur)—an instrument that detects physical changes in the environment

sweep angle (SWEEP ANG-guhl)—the wing angle of an airplane; wing angle affects the speed of an aircraft.

swing-wing (SWING-WING)—the ability to move a plane's wings forward or backward

thrust (THRUST)—the force created by a jet engine; thrust pushes an airplane forward.

To Learn More

Chant, Christopher. *Role of the Fighter and Bomber.* The World's Greatest Aircraft. Philadelphia: Chelsea House, 2000.

Holden, Henry M. *Navy Combat Aircraft and Pilots.* Aircraft. Berkeley Heights, N.J.: Enslow, 2002.

Maynard, Christopher. *Aircraft.* The Need for Speed. Minneapolis: Lerner, 1999.

Useful Addresses

National Museum of Naval Aviation
1750 Radford Boulevard
Pensacola, FL 32508

Naval Air Systems Command
Public Affairs Department
47123 Buse Road
Building 2272, Unit IPT
Patuxent River, MD 20670-1647

Internet Sites

Do you want to find out more about F-14 Tomcats?
Let FactHound, our fact-finding hound dog, do the research
for you.

Here's how:
1) Visit *http://www.facthound.com.*
2) Type in the **Book ID** number: **073682149X**
3) Click on **FETCH IT**

FactHound will fetch Internet sites
picked by our editors just for you!

Index

AIM-7 Sparrow, 22
AIM-9 Sidewinder, 22
AIM-54 Phoenix, 20–21
APG-71, 15
AWG-9, 14, 15

engines, 12

F/A-18 Super Hornet, 27
FLIR, 25

Global Positioning
    System, 25

head-up display, 14

IRST, 28

LANTIRN, 25
laser-guided bombs, 22

M61A1 Vulcan, 23

night vision goggles, 28
Northrop Grumman, 7, 8

swing-wing, 12

TV Camera System, 28

variable-geometry, 12